MW01679991

Letters and Reflections

to My Adopted Daughters

Letters and Reflections

to My Adopted Daughters

Penned by John Newton,
writer of the hymn, Amazing Grace

Compiled by Jody Moreen

Pleasant Word
A Division of WINEPRESS PUBLISHING

Printed in the United States of America

Packaged by Pleasant Word, a division of WinePress Publishing, PO Box 428, Enumclaw, WA 98022. The views expressed or implied in this work do not necessarily reflect those of Pleasant Word, a division of WinePress Publishing. Ultimate design, content, and editorial accuracy of this work are the responsibilities of the author.

Unless otherwise noted, all Scriptures are taken from the King James Version of the Bible.

ISBN 1-4141-0264-X
Library of Congress Catalog Card Number: 2004096292

Table of Contents

Foreword

It is with great joy that I share these letters and reflections penned in the 1700s by John Newton, the famous writer of the hymn *Amazing Grace*. I pray that as you read them you will be encouraged and inspired as you witness the tender heart of this godly father. Though he and his wife, Polly, were childless, he embraced the role of parent that God entrusted to him. He adopted his two orphaned nieces, Elizabeth Catlett and Eliza Cunningham.

John Newton was a well-known pastor who for forty-three years shepherded two churches in Olney and London, England. As busy as he was, he did not neglect to take the time to disciple his daughters in the ways of God. In a letter penned to Elizabeth when she was away at college he wrote:

My Dear Child,

You may well expect to hear from me; but you will hardly expect a long letter, if you remember what little leisure I have in London. Almost every day loads me with debt, and brings me letters which I am not able to answer; but my dear Betsy must not be forgotten." (Letter 2) Newtons' letters in this volume reveal the passion he had to faithfully instruct his children in the ways of the Lord and reveal his character to them. This book combines two tracts written by Newton, both published by The American Tract Society in the 1800s. Both contain treasures of wisdom and counsel that will not only encourage parents, but youth as well. He intentionally addressed youth at the conclusion of the narrative of Eliza Cunningham. His sincere hope was that they would heed his exhortation to embrace their Savior, Jesus Christ while they were young.

The first tract, *Letters to an Adopted Daughter*, contain twenty-one letters written to his daughter Elizabeth. These letters are filled with affection, godly counsel, and edification. The second half of the book shares Newton's memoirs of his younger daughter, Eliza. His recollections in this narrative focus on Eliza's virtue and exemplary faith displayed in the final weeks of her short fourteen-year life. She died from complications of tuberculosis. Newton shared his insights and personal emotions from this difficult, but enlightening journey. He continually shined a light on the promise of eternal life for those that accept Christ as Savior.

As I read these heartfelt letters and memoirs, I felt a bit of nostalgia for the bygone days of handwritten letters. Letters that were thoughtfully composed, often on special stationery or parchment, some even scented, penned with a special fountain pen or ink, signed in cursive, and stamped with an embossed seal. Letters that were cherished and saved, and often passed down as a legacy to loved ones. Electronic mail, though fast and efficient, pales in comparison with the beautiful vanishing art of letter writing. I hope that some who read this book may be motivated to visit their local stationery store. Take some time to browse through their fine stationery offerings, choose and purchase some pretty paper, find that old fountain pen laying idle in your desk drawer, and write a letter to your child or that special someone!

God's blessings,

Jody Moreen, A twice adopted daughter;
by my parents and by my heavenly
Father

Introduction

The Rev. John Newton, author of the following letters, was one of the most estimable men that have adorned any age. His interesting memoir, which may be found among the publications of the American Tract Society, exhibits a most eventful life. Nearly forty years he lived in sin and folly and consequent misery; but he then became an able and evangelical minister of Christ, first for fourteen years in Olney, where, in connexion with the poet Cowper he published the excellent "Olney Hymns," and then for twenty-eight years in London. His published works comprise six volumes of great value.

In Mrs. Newton he had a companion of kindred spirit; and as they had no children, they adopted two of Mrs. Newton's nieces, Elizabeth Catlett and Eliza Cunningham. Miss Cunningham died at an early age, and Mr. Newton perpetuated the memory of her piety and virtue in a brief memoir, which is remarkable for the beautiful simplicity of its style and the loveliness of the character which it delineates. See Tract No. 83

To the other niece, Miss Catlett, the following pleasing effusions of Mr. Newton's affectionate heart were addressed while she was absent from them at school. They cannot fail to engage the attention of the young; they contain suggestions and counsel of great value, whether regard be had to the present or a future life.

It is interesting to know that these instructive admonitions were not lost upon the young person to whom they were addressed. She became a truly pious and estimable woman, and the latter years of her venerable relative were cheered by her grateful and devoted attentions. After the death of his wife and Miss Cunningham she became his daily companion, anticipated his wants and wishes, read to him when his eye-sight failed, took care of him in sickness, and conducted towards him in all respects as a dutiful and affectionate daughter.

Letter 1

Olney, September 8, 1779.

My Dear Child,

I was glad of your letter, for we were just thinking of you, as it seems you were of us, that it was a long time since we heard from you. When you want a letter from me, you must write; if I send you one for one, I think it will be pretty well.

R.**** died about a fortnight ago, and I buried him and three others within a week. All four were rather young people, that is about thirty years of age. Last Sabbath evening I preached a funeral sermon for Richard; the text was, Gen. 49:19, "A troop shall overcome him, but he shall overcome at the last." That short verse contained his history; and I hope it contains yours likewise. The first part is sure to you if you live; you will meet with many troops—sins, fears, cares, and troubles—which will fight against you, and seem at times almost to overcome you; yea, overcome you they certainly would, if you were to fight them in your own strength. If you should not seek and love the Lord Jesus, you would be destroyed by them. But I cannot bear to entertain such a thought; surely you must, you will love him. You hear a great deal of his beauty and goodness; believe it, for it is true, and remember that a great deal is but little of what ought to be said of him. But pray him to show himself and his own love to your heart; then you would love him indeed: all the world would love him, did they but rightly know him. Well, if you love the Lord Jesus you will certainly overcome at last; and then you shall have the crown of life, and all the happiness which is contained in the promises made to them who overcome, in the second and third chapters of Revelation. My dear child, pray to him, and never be content or satisfied till you feel your desire and love fixed upon him. Nothing less will content me for you. If you should behave to me and your mamma with the greatest tenderness, affection and attention, as you grow up, (as I hope you will, and you yourself are sensible you ought,) still I should weep over you if I saw you negligent and ungrateful towards the Lord. We love you, and would do much to show our love; but we could not, we dare not be crucified for you. This was such love as only he could show; judge what a return it calls for from you. Not to love the Lord, is an evidence of the height of wickedness, and the depth of misery.

Believe me to be yours.

Letter 1

Letter 2

Old Jewry, Oct. 22, 1779.

My Dear Child,

You may well expect to hear from me; but you will hardly expect a long letter, if you remember what little leisure I have in London. Almost every day loads me with debt, and brings me letters which I am not able to answer; but my dear Betsy must not be forgotten. We have been here a fortnight and upwards; the Lord gave us a pleasant and safe journey. Your mamma has been, upon the whole, comfortably well; and as we are at Dr. ****'s I need not tell you that we are situated as much to our minds as we can be in the midst of so much noise and smoke. But here I can have no garden—no pretty walks among trees and fields—no birds but such as are prisoners in iron cages, so that I pity them, for all their singing.

But the same sun that shines at N**** is often to be seen at London; and the Lord Jesus, like the sun, is in all places at once. Go where we will, we are not far from him, if we have but eyes to see him and hearts to perceive him. My dear child, when you look at the sun I wish it may lead your thoughts to him who made it, and who placed it in the firmament, not only to give us light, but to be the brightest, noblest emblem of himself; there is but one sun, and there needs not another; so there is but one Savior; but he is complete and all-sufficient, the Sun of righteousness, the fountain of life and comfort; his beams, wherever they reach, bring healing, strength, peace, and joy to the soul. Pray to him, my dear, to shine forth and reveal himself to you. O how different is he from all that you have ever seen with your bodily eyes! He is the sun of the soul, and he can make you as sensible of his presence as you are of the sunshine at noonday; and when once you obtain a clear sight of him, a thousand little things which have hitherto engaged your attention, will, in a manner, disappear.

As by the light of op'ning day
The stars are all conceal'd;
So earthly beauties fade away
When Jesus is reveal'd.

I entreat, I charge you to ask him every day to show himself to you. Think of him as being always with you; about your path by day, about your bed by night; nearer to you than any object you can see, though you see him not; whether you are sitting or walking, in company or alone. People often consider God as if he saw them from a great distance; but this is wrong, for though he be in heaven, the heaven of heavens cannot contain him; he is as much with us as with the angels; in him we live and move and have our being, as we live in the air which surrounds us, and is within us, so that it cannot be separated from us a moment. And whatever thoughts you can obtain of God from the Scripture, as great, holy, wise, and good, endeavor to apply them all to Jesus Christ, who once died upon the cross; for he is the true God and eternal life, with whom you have to do; and though he be the King of kings and Lord of lords and rules over all, he is so condescending and compassionate that he will hear and answer the prayer of a child. Seek him, and you shall find him; whatever else you seek, you may be disappointed; but he is never sought in vain.

Your very affectionate father.

Letter 3

Charles Sq. Hoxton, April 8, 1780.

My Dear Child,

I have heard of you several times since I received your letter, which I wished to answer before. I would be thankful that you are well, and I hope you are happy, that is, in the common sense of the word; for, strictly speaking, happiness is not to be found here. I hope, however, you are cheerful, thankful, and in some degree satisfied with your lot; and, in order to this, I would wish you to look round you, and see how many children are sick, while you are well—poor and destitute, while you are provided not only with the necessaries, but the comforts of life. How many, again, are exposed to hard and unkind treatment; whereas you are noticed and caressed, and have kind friends abroad and at home. Once more, consider how many are brought up in ignorance and wickedness, having nothing but evil examples, and it is to be feared will go from bad to worse as they grow up; while you have the advantage of good education and good examples, and are placed where you can hear the precious Gospel, by which the Lord gives faith and salvation to them that seek him. Then ask yourself how it is, or why you are better off than they? And I hope there is something within you that will tell you, whatever the reason may be, it is not because you are better in yourself, or deserve better things than others. Your heart is no better; you likewise are a sinner; you were born with a sinful disposition, and, though you are a child, you have sinned against the Lord; so that had he been strict to mark what is amiss, he might justly have cut you off long ago. The reason why you are so favored, must be the Lord's mercy and goodness. He pitied you when you did not know how to pity yourself; and in his providence he removed you from a place where you would probably have remained ignorant of him, and he placed you under our care, and made you dear to us, that we might feel a pleasure in doing every thing in our power to promote your welfare. And I hope that you and we shall have reason to thank him that you came to us.

The days are growing long, the summer is coming, and among the many pleasant days of summer there is one which I hope will bring you home. I believe you will be glad to come, and we shall be glad to see you: I hope you will like the house. There are green trees in front, and a green field back, with cows feeding in it; so that it has some little resemblance of the country.

Your mamma desired Miss **** to send you a cake, which I hope you received; and if you did, I suppose it is all gone by this time; for you cannot eat your cake and have it. It is a true saying and full of meaning. Look at all that appears good and pleasant in this world; could you call it all your own, it would last but a little while, and when you go into another world, the remembrance of what you had in this will be but like remembering you once had a cake, but it is gone, quite eaten up. But it is not so, my dear child, with respect to that feast which Jesus prepares for poor sinners. The pleasures which he gives are repeated from time to time, and are pleasing even when we reflect on them. And in the other world, when earthly pleasures will be quite ended, they that love him shall have pleasure without interruption and without end, rivers of pleasure at his right hand for evermore. The Lord bless you, and keep you. It is one of my pleasures while here, to think of you, to feel for you, and to write to you, as

Your affectionate.

Letter 4

August 3, 1780.

My Dear Child,

You may be sure your mamma and I were very glad to hear that the Lord preserved you from harm, and that you were safe and well at N****. I wish you to have a deep impression on your mind, that your safety, whether abroad or at home, or the continuance of your health from one hour to another, is not a matter of course, but the effect of the care and goodness of Him who knows we are helpless as sheep, and condescends to act the part of a shepherd towards us. May you love to acknowledge him in all your ways, to pray to him for his blessing, and to praise him daily for his mercies; and then you will do well. This is the great privilege which distinguishes us from the beasts of the field; they likewise owe their preservation to his providence;

but then they are not capable of knowing him or thanking him. There are many young people who are contented to live without God in this world; but this is not only their sin, but their shame likewise. They thereby renounce the chief honor they are capable of, and degrade themselves to a level with the brute creation. But let it not be so with you. Pray to the Lord to teach you to love him, and when you think of him, fix your thoughts upon Jesus Christ; upon him who conversed on earth as a man. The great God has manifested himself in a way suited to us, as weak creatures and poor sinners.

God is everywhere present, but only those who look to him in Christ can love, trust, or serve him aright. When you read our Savior's discourses recorded by the Evangelists, attend as if you saw him with your own eyes standing before you; and when you try to pray, assure yourself before you begin, that he is actually in the room with you, and that his ear is open to every word you say. This will make you serious, and it will likewise encourage you, when you consider that you are not speaking into the air, or to one who is a great way off, but to One who is very near you—to your best friend, who is both able and willing to give you every thing that is good for you.

Though you have not been gone from us a fortnight, we seem too long to see you again. August is come already; and December, which we hope will bring you to us again, will be here before long. I shall be glad if you make the best of your time, and return so much improved that we may be able to keep you at home; for it is no pleasure to us to have you at such a distance from us. But there is no suitable day-school in this neighborhood, and if you must be at a boarding-school, I believe you must be at N****; for after you have been so long there, we should not be willing to take you from Mrs. ****'s school to put you to another; it would seem a slight to her; though our motive would be only to have you nearer to us, people would think we had other reasons.

My advice to you will be chiefly with respect to your religious concerns and your moral conduct. But there are other things belonging to your mamma's province. She wishes, as you grow up, you may not appear to a disadvantage when compared with other young women; and indeed, if you should be every thing she wishes you to be, you will do honor to the school you come from.

* * * * * *

I think you are in general willing to oblige her, and I am persuaded a little care and resolution on your part would soon make it easy and familiar to you to follow the example she sets you, as well as the advice she gives you. I hope, therefore, for her sake, for mine, for the sake of your governess, and especially for your own sake, you will endeavor to make the best improvement of your time. It was a grief to me that my time was so unavoidably taken up that I could spare but little to converse with you; but we agreed, you know, to make it up by letters. It is now your turn to write, and I shall be glad of a long letter from you soon, in which I wish you to open your mind, to tell me what you think, feel, hope, fear, or desire, with the same freedom as if you were writing to one of your school-fellows.

The Lord bless you, my dear child, and cause you to increase in wisdom and grace, as you increase in years. Always think of me as

Your very affectionate father.

Letter 5

November 1, 1780.

My Dear Child,

I congratulate you that you are now within a month of December, when you will begin to count the days, and see the vacation peeping over the head of a short interval. I may congratulate your mamma, and myself likewise, (provided you come to us improved as we wish you,) for we long to see you, and have done so every day since you left us.

Your mamma is often indisposed, but seldom very ill, at least, not long together; but both she and I have many feelings with which we were not acquainted when we were young like you. The advantages of youth and health are seldom rightly known at the right time. It is indeed a mercy, if, when we are growing old, we have some proper sense of the folly and vanity we indulged in early life, and can be ashamed as we ought, to think how many opportunities we neglected, how many talents we misimproved. Yet repentance cannot recall the day that is past. It is my frequent prayer, that you may be wiser than I was at your time of life, that you may have grace to remember your Creator and Redeemer while you are yet young. Depend upon it, my dear, whenever you really know the Lord, you will be sorry you did not know him sooner; whenever you experience that pleasure which is only to be found in loving and serving him, you will wish you had loved and served him (if possible) from your very cradle.

I have no news to tell you; but one thing I can assure you, which, though you have often heard, I hope the repetition will be always pleasing to you—I mean, that I am your very affectionate friend, and feel for you as if I was really and truly your father.

Letter 6

January 10, 1781.

My Dear Child,

I tell many of my friends abroad, that my time is so much taken up they must not expect me to write to them; and yet I have offered to begin a new correspondence with you, though you are in the same house with me. I would have you take notice, and I believe you will, of this, as well as of other circumstances by which, as occasions offer, I take a pleasure in showing you that I dearly love you, and long to contribute every thing in my power to your improvement and to your satisfaction; and I persuade myself, the hope I form of a suitable return of love and attention from you will not be disappointed. The Lord, in his good providence, gave you to me as a gift, and committed you to me as a trust;

at the same time, he gave me a great love for you: and whatever we do for those we love, we do with pleasure.

I thank you for your letter of yesterday. It encourages me to hope that the gracious Savior is knocking at the door of your heart. I doubt not but you write what you think and feel, yet there is more meaning in your expressions than either you or I can fully comprehend. You are, as you say, a sinner; a young sinner, and yet a great sinner. It is not your case alone—we are all born in sin; but to be sensible that you are a sinner, is a mercy afforded but to few children at your age. May the Lord keep the persuasion alive in your heart. But the word sinner includes so much, that a whole long life will hardly suffice to give you a full sense of it. Thus much I hope you know already, that a sinner needs a Savior; and that Jesus is the Savior of all sinners that seek him. I commend you to him; if he has taught you a little, he will teach you more. Put yourself simply into his hand, trust alone in his mercy; he works powerfully, but for the most part gently and gradually. You know the sun does not break upon us all at once in the dark night; there is first a glimmering dawn in the sky, which gives us notice that he is coming, and prepares us for his appearance. By degrees that faint light grows brighter; we see clearer and farther; it becomes broad day, and after that the sun rises.

Your part is to pray to him, to hear his word, and to listen with attention when you hear it preached. I trust you will find your light increase, and difficulties abate. I wish you to be as cheerful and easy as possible. Cheerfulness is no sin, nor is there any grace in a solemn cast of countenance. On the other hand, I would not have you light or giddy with levity; it will hurt your own spirit, and hinder you from the pursuit of what in your serious moments you most desire. I know your natural spirits are changeable; sometimes they are highly volatile: I would have you correct them, by thinking you are a sinner. Sometimes you are grave enough; but if you feel uneasy, then try to think what a Savior is offered to you. Be sure you do not indulge a hard thought of him, as though he were severe and stern, and ready to take advantage of you. Form your ideas of him from the accounts the Evangelists give you, that he was meek and lowly when upon earth, full of compassion and gentleness, ready to pity, to heal, to help, and to teach all who come to him; and they will tell you that he had great love for children. He tells you so himself. You read how he took them in his arms, put his hands on them, and blessed them. When you think of this, speak to him in your heart, and say, Lord, bless me too.

One of the best methods of keeping free from uneasy, troublesome thoughts, at least of lessening them, is to be always employed; strive and pray against indolence, look upon it as a hurtful, yea, a sinful thing. Read in English and French, write and work. Your mamma and I will be both willing you should diversify these employments as may be most agreeable to your own inclination; but we wish not to see you idle. Now is the time of life for you to acquire useful knowledge, that you may make yourself agreeable, and that you may be useful and qualified to fill that station in the world which the Lord may allot you. I will gladly assist you as much as I can in what falls under my department; but you know I have but little time. God has given you a good capacity, and therefore the less assistance will be necessary, if you are not wanting to yourself. You may depend on our doing what we can to make you happy. If we seem to cross your wishes sometimes, or not to comply with your desire, you may be sure we have some reason for it. You shall go out with us as often as we shall think it proper and right; and we shall not leave you at home for our own pleasure, but because it would not be good for you to be very much abroad. We expect and hope you will be ruled by a hint or a word; and then you will find us studious in contriving how to make every thing as agreeable as possible to you. Because you desired a letter soon, I have written thus early, although I had to preach this morning, and other things to do. I shall hope for a letter from you very earnestly. The Lord bless you. I am, my dear child,

Your affectionate father.

Letter 7

October 17, 1781.

My Dear Child,

I send you the first letter; in future you must not expect me to write but in answer to yours. We wish to hear soon that you are well, and that you like your situation. I do not wish you to like any place so well as home; upon one account you ought not; for it is impossible any persons should ever love you so well as your mamma and I do; and therefore you are bound to love us dearly, and that will make you love home; and the more you love home, the more diligent you will be in the improvement of your time at school. For your return to us must in a great measure depend upon yourself; it is no pleasure to us to send you abroad. I thought for a day or two the house looked vacant without you, and I miss you a little every day still; but we are forced to part with you for your own good.

I cannot bear the thoughts of your growing up like a tall weed; I want you to appear like a pretty flower; and it is observable that the best of flowers in a garden would in time degenerate into tawdry weeds, if they were not cultivated; such is the importance of education to children. The Lord has been good to you; he has given you good understanding and natural abilities—and much that is engaging in your disposition. It would be a great pity that, with all these advantages, you should prove only a weed. To prevent it, I was obliged to transplant you from London to H****, where I hope you will thrive and flourish, increasing in wisdom and favor as you increase in stature.

I have written you many letters in a religious strain, which I hope you have preserved, and will now and then read them over, the more willingly, perhaps, because your papa wrote them. I would not weary you with this subject; though the truth is, this is my chief desire for you that you may know the Lord and love him; if not, though you were accomplished and admired beyond any of your age, and though you could live in all the splendor of a queen, I should weep over you; I should lament your birth, and the day when you first came under my care. But I know that I cannot make you truly religious, nor can you, without Divine aid, make yourself so. It is the Lord's work, and I am daily praying him to bless you indeed. I hope you will wait upon him, according to your light, in the use of his appointed means, that you will make conscience of praying to him, of reading his Word, and of hearing it when you have opportunity. I hope he will enable you to behave obediently and affectionately to your governess, and in an obliging manner to all around you, so as to gain their love and esteem. I hope you will likewise carefully abstain from whatever you know to be wrong. Thus far I may hope you can go at present; but I do not wish you to affect more of religion in your appearance than you are really conscious of possessing. There is some danger of this in a family where a religious profession is countenanced. Young people are apt to imitate those about them, and sometimes (which is abominable) to put on a show of religion in order to please, though their hearts have no concern in it. I have a good hope that the Lord will teach you and guide you, and that the many prayers I have offered on your behalf will not be lost.

When I began my letter I did not mean to write half so gravely, I rather thought to find something to divert you; but you are very near my heart, and this makes me serious. I long to come and see you; but it cannot be yet, nor can I say when; but I shall bounce in upon you some day, when perhaps you are not thinking of me.

I am, my dear,
Your very affectionate.

Letter 8

November 10, 1781.

My Dear Child,

When your mamma and I come to see you, it must be on a Monday, for more reasons than one, which it is not necessary for you to know; and as there is but one Monday in a week, something or other may prevent oftener than I wish. However, I promise to think of you when I cannot see you, and sometimes we talk of you. "Christmas will soon be here; then we shall have her at home, and then who knows but she will be so improved, and behave so nicely, that we shall be sorry to part with her again." Since we talk thus, I hope you will make good what we say.

Lately, for about a week, I was attacked by a company of pains. Some seized my face and teeth, some took possession of my back, and some got into my sides; but they are all gone now, and they did me no harm. You know little about pains and cares yet. You are now at the time of life when you are especially called upon to remember your Creator, and have the greatest advantages for doing it. But if your life is spared, to you likewise the days will come when you will say, "I have no pleasure in them." But I hope, long before they come, you will have some experience of pleasures which do not at all depend upon youth or health, or any thing that this world can either give or take away.

Seek the Lord, and you shall live; and you have not far to seek for him; he is very near you; he is all around you; about your bed by night, and your path by day. He sees, he notices all you say and do. But I do not wish you to conceive of him so as to make the thought of him uneasy to you. Think of him according to the account the Evangelists give of him when he was upon earth; how gracious, compassionate, and kind he was. If he were upon earth now, would you not wish that I should lead you to him, that he might lay his hands upon you and bless you, as he did the children which were brought to him? If he were here, and I could go with you and say, "Lord, bless my child likewise!" I am sure he would not frown at you, and say, "Take her away, I will have nothing to do with her!" No, my dear child, he has promised, them that come to him he will in no wise cast out. Go to him yourself; though you cannot see him, it is sufficient that he sees and hears you. Tell him that you hear and believe he is a Savior to many, and beg him to be your Savior too. Tell him it was not your own choice, but his providence that removed you from C**** and put you under my care, which gave you an opportunity of knowing more of his goodness than you would otherwise have done; and beg of him to give you his grace, that the advantages you have had may not aggravate your sins, but lead you to his salvation; and do not let a day pass without thinking on his sufferings in Gethsemane and on Golgotha. Surely his love to poor sinners, in bleeding and dying for them, will constrain you to love him again; and if once you love him, then everything will be easy, and you will account it your greatest pleasure to please him.

I thank you for your letter: I conceive a hope from it, that you will improve in your writing. I wish you not only to write a good hand but a good letter; and the whole art is to write with freedom and ease. When you take your pen in hand, put things down just as they come to your mind—just as you would speak of them without study. Tell me something about the fowls in the yard, or the trees in the garden, or what you please; only write freely. The Lord bless you; I love you dearly, and wish you to believe me to be,

Your affectionate.

Letter 9

My Dear Child,

Mrs. **** died on the Fast-day, and was buried yesterday. I had often visited her during her illness, and was at her funeral. She was well a few months ago, but a consumption soon brought her down to the grave. But though she was young, she was not sorry to leave such a poor world as this. I always found her happy and cheerful, though her illness was very painful. She suffered much by cold sweats; but she said, a few days before her death, that it would be worth lying a thousand years in a cold sweat, for one hour's happiness such as she then felt. "Oh!" she said, "if this be dying, what a pleasant thing dying is."

I think, my dear child, you have told me that you are often terrified at the thoughts of death; now, if you seek the Lord, as Mrs. **** did, while you are young, then, whenever you come to die you will find that death has nothing terrible in it to them that love the Lord Jesus Christ. He has disarmed death and taken away its sting; and he has promised to meet his people and receive them to himself, when they are about to leave this world and everything they loved in it behind them. You have the same advantages that Mrs. **** had; like her, you are placed under the care of those who wish well to your soul; the Scriptures, which made her wise to salvation, are put into your hand likewise, and you also have the opportunity of hearing the Gospel. She was exhorted and encouraged, from a child, to pray to the Lord for his grace; and so are you. I hope you will do as she did; and the Lord, who was gracious to her, will be gracious to you; for he has promised that none who seek him, shall seek him in vain.

Your conscience tells you that you are a sinner, and that makes you afraid; but when the Lord gives you faith you will see and understand that the blood of Jesus Christ cleanses from all sin; then you will love him; and when you love him you will find it easy and pleasant to serve him; and then you will long to see him who died for you; and as it is impossible to see him in this world, you will be glad that you are not to stay here always; you will be willing to die, that you may be with him where he is. In the mean time I hope you will pray to him, trusting that he will reveal himself to you; endeavoring to avoid whatever you know to be wrong and displeasing to him; and sometimes, I hope, you will feel your heart soft and tender, and serious thoughts and desires rising in your mind; when you do, then think,

"Now is the Lord calling me!" and say, as Samuel did, "Speak, Lord, for thy servant heareth." He does not call with an audible voice, but he speaks to the heart in a way not to be described by words. When we are grieved and ashamed for our sins; when we are afflicted with what we read and hear of him, of his love, his sufferings, and his death; when we see and feel that nothing but his favor can make us happy; then we may be sure the Lord is near.

I believe you have too much sense and honesty to make a profession of religion, further than your heart is really engaged, in order to please your fellow-creatures. But, on the other hand, I would not have you backward to open your mind to me on religious subjects. I know you are not without convictions, and though all convictions are not right, yet true religion always begins with convictions. We must know we are sick before we can prize a physician. If I live to see you a partaker of the grace of God, one of the chief desires of my heart will be gratified: This would please me more than to have your weight in gold, and therefore you may be sure I often pray for you.

I am your affectionate.

Letter 10

August 1, 1782.

My Dear Child,

Do not think we forget you: Our love would reach you were you a hundred times further from us than Highgate is; but we are very much taken up. Monday your mamma was ill in bed all day; she is pretty well now, but P**** is very bad indeed, worse I believe than ever you saw her, and we can hardly attend to anything but her. Then again poor Mr. B**** was hurt by a mad ox, about ten days since; his life has been in great danger, but we now hope he will recover. I visit him every day, and that takes up a good deal of my time.

I would be thankful that the Lord preserves you in health and safety. I hope you are thankful too. When you see any body sick, or hurt, or lame, I would have you think it is of the Lord's goodness their case is not yours. Sin has filled the world with sorrow; all the calamities you read or hear of, or see with your eyes, are the fruits of sin; and as you are a sinner, you might suffer what others do, and it is only the Lord's mercy that preserves you, and provides you good things which many others have not. You know many children are brought up in poverty, meet with ill treatment, have no parents or kind friends to take care of them. But though the Lord removed your parents before you were old enough to miss them, he took care to provide you a place with us; he inclined us not only to receive you but to love you; and now your wants are all supplied: besides this, you have been instructed, and prayed for every day. You have great reason to be thankful indeed, and I hope you will pray to the Lord to give you a thankful heart; for you cannot have it except he gives it you. That hymn in Dr. Watts' little book—

Whene'er I take my walks abroad, &c.

Though it is written principally for children, will deserve your notice when you grow up and become a woman: I hope you will say from your heart,

Not more than others I deserve,
Yet God has give me more.

Oh, it is a great blessing to be sensible we deserve nothing from God but misery, and that all the good we receive is mercy; and then to know that all this mercy we owe to the Lord Jesus, who died for us that we might live and be happy.

There's ne'er a gift his hand bestows,
But cost his heart a groan.

When you understand this you will love him, and then you will be happy indeed; then it will be your pleasure to please him, and then, putting your trust in him, you will be preserved from anxiety and evil.

Your affectionate.

Letter 11

August 10, 1782.

My Dear Child,

"Vanity of vanities!" saith the preacher — "How vain are all things here below!" saith Dr. Watts: and you and I, and your mamma, may say so likewise; for we all counted upon meeting you last Sabbath: We listened at the door and peeped out of the window, but no Betsy came. When we heard by Miss **** that you were well, we were satisfied. Now we will venture to expect you next Sabbath. Indeed it is not amiss that you should now and then meet with a disappointment, that you may learn, if possible, not to count too much on what to-morrow may do for you; and that you may begin to feel the impossibility of being happy any further than your will is brought into submission to the will of God. In order to this, you must have your own will frequently crossed; and things do and will turn out, almost daily, in one way or other, contrary to our wishes and expectations. Then some people fret and fume, are angry and impatient; but others who are in the Lord's school, and desirous of being taught by him, get good by these things, and sometimes find more pleasure in yielding to his appointment, though contrary to their own wills, than they would have found if all had happened just to their wish.

I wish you, my dear child, to think much of the Lord's governing providence. It extends to the minutest concerns. He rules and manages all things, but in so secret a way that most people think he does nothing, when, in reality, he does all. He appointed the time of your coming into the world; and the day and hour of your coming from Highgate to us depends upon him likewise: nor can you come in safety one step of the road without his protection and care over you. It may now seem a small matter to you and to me, whether you came home last Sabbath or are to come home next Sabbath: But we know not what different consequences may depend upon the day: We know not what hidden danger you might escape by staying at Highgate last Sabbath. The Lord knows all things; he foresees every possible consequence; and often what we call disappointments are mercies from him to save us from harm.

If I could teach you a lesson which as yet I have but poorly learned myself, I would put you in a way that you should never be disappointed. This would be the case, if you could always form a right judgment of this world, and all things in it. If you go to a blackberry bush to look for grapes, you must be disappointed; but then you must thank yourself, for you are big enough to know that grapes never grow upon brambles. So if you expect much pleasure here, you will not find it; but you ought not to say you are disappointed, because the Scripture warned you beforehand to look for crosses, trials, and disappointments, every day. If you expect such things, you will not be disappointed when they happen.

I am your very affectionate.

Letter 12

October 15, 1782.

My Dear Child,

It is rather to your disadvantage I have lately corrected a mistake I had made. I thought you were but twelve years old last birthday; but I read in a blank leaf of the great Bible, that my child was born June 22, 1769; consequently you are now in your fourteenth year. Therefore, to keep pace with my ideas and wishes, you ought to be a whole year more advanced in improvements of every kind than you are; a whole year wiser. Some things which I might think very tolerable in my child, supposing she was but twelve years old, will seem but rather so so, when I know she is thirteen; and some things of another sort will be quite unsuitable at the age of thirteen which might be more excusable if you were but twelve. You see, my dear child, you must use double diligence to fetch up this year, which we have somehow lost out of the account. You have a year less for improvement, and are a year nearer to the time in which you will begin to appear like a young woman, than I expected. I know not but I should have been pleased to find that I had made a mistake on the other side, and that you were a year younger than I had supposed you. As it is, I shall hope the best; I do not complain of you. As I love you dearly, so I have much comfort in you; and I trust you will pray to the Lord for yourself, as I do for you, that he may give you grace, and wisdom, and blessing; then I know you will do well. But sometimes, when I consider what a world you are growing up into, and what snares and dangers young people are exposed to, with little experience to help them, I have some painful feelings for you.

The other day I was at Deptford, and saw a ship launched: She slipped easily into the water; the people on board shouted; the ship looked clean and gay; she was fresh painted, and her colors flying. But I looked at her with a sort of pity: "Poor ship," I thought, "you are now in port and in safety, but ere long you must go to sea. Who can tell what storms you may meet with hereafter, and to what hazards you may be exposed; how weather-beaten you may be before you return to port again, or whether you may return at all!" Then my thoughts turned from the ship to my child. It seemed an emblem of your present state: You are now, as it were, in a safe harbor; but by and by you must launch out into the world, which may well be compared to a tempestuous sea. I could even now almost weep at the resemblance; but I take courage; my hopes are greater than my fears. I know there is an infallible Pilot, who has the winds and the waves at his command. There is hardly a day passes in which I do not entreat him to take charge of you. Under his care I know you will be safe; he can guide you unhurt amidst the storms, and rocks, and dangers by which you might otherwise suffer, and bring you at last to the haven of eternal rest. I hope you will seek him while you are young, and I am sure he will be the friend of them that seek him sincerely: Then you will be happy, and I shall rejoice. Nothing will satisfy me but this; though I should live to see you settled to the greatest advantage in temporal matters, except you love him and live in his fear and favor, you would appear to me quite miserable. I think it would go near to break my heart; for, next to your dear mamma, there is nothing so dear to me in this world as you. But the Lord gave you to me, and I have given you to him again, many and many a time upon my knees, and therefore I hope you must, and will, and shall be his.

I hardly know any accomplishment I more wish you to obtain, than a talent of writing free and easy letters; and I am ready to think, if you could freely open your mind to me, you might inform me of something I should be glad to know, or you might propose to me some things which now and then trouble your thoughts, and thereby give me an opportunity of attempting to relieve, encourage, or direct you. For these reasons I have requested of your governess to permit you now and then to seal up your letters to me or your mamma without showing them to her. I have asked this liberty for you, only when you write to us; nor even then always, but at such times as you find yourself disposed to write more freely than you could do if your letters were to be seen before you send them. I have likewise told her that I would desire you to be as careful in writing as if she was to see your letters, and not send us pothooks and hangers, as they say, because you know she will not inspect your writing. Under these restrictions, she has promised to oblige me; and I take it as a favor, for I am well aware that, in general, it is by no means proper that young people at school should write letters from thence without the knowledge of their governess. But yours has so good an opinion of you and of me, that she is willing to trust us, and I hope we shall neither of us make an improper use of her indulgence. I am, with great tenderness,

My dear child,
Your verv affectionate father.

Letter 13

January 27, 1783.

My Dear Child,

Want of leisure, and not want of inclination, prevented my writing before you left home; and I now take the first opportunity that has offered since you went from us. If I had no more correspondents than you have, you would hear from me very often; nor can I expect to hear from you so often as I wish, because I consider you likewise have your engagements; and though, perhaps, I am not willing to allow that your business is as important as some of mine, it must and ought for the present to take up a good deal of your time. You have not only reading and writing and arithmetic to mind, but you work sprigs and flowers, and maps, and cut bits of paper to pieces, and learn a strange language, so that you are very busy to be sure;

and it is best for you, for idleness and sauntering are very great evils, and doors by which a thousand temptations and mischiefs may enter.

Your mamma and I are well pleased with you, on the whole; your affection is not lost upon us; we think we can perceive an improvement in you, and, we believe, the things in which you yet fail, proceed rather from inattention than from the want of a desire to please: And we have a good hope that, as you grow older, you will outgrow that heedlessness which you sometimes discover. You are not yet a woman, but neither are you a child; you are almost fourteen, and at that age a certain degree of thought and forecast may be hoped for which it would have been unreasonable to expect from you some few years ago. It has pleased God to give you a capacity for improvement; and, as you see we are so situated that neither your mamma nor I can bestow that time and attention upon you, when you are at home, which we would wish, I hope you will make the best use you possibly can of the opportunities you have at school. It is no pleasure to us that you should live so much from us, for we love you dearly, and love your company; but it is what we submit to for your advantage.

You desired me to send you news, when I should write; but I have little to tell you. The public news you will hear, I suppose, from twenty people; it is very important. The Lord is about to give us the blessing of peace. Neither you nor I can tell the value of this blessing, because we have not known the want of it. It is true, we have heard much talk of war, and we have heard of the calamities which war has occasioned; but we have heard of them as things which have happened at a distance: Had we lived in America we should probably have seen and felt them. We should have seen towns, villages, and houses in flames; have heard the groans of widows and orphans around us; have had every thing we call our own torn from us, and perhaps have been glad to hide ourselves in the woods to save ourselves. Such has been the lot of thousands in the course of the war.

If you remember the hurry, confusion, and terror which prevailed at the time of the riots, it may give you some apprehension of the case of those who live in a country which is the seat of war. Our apprehensions were over in a few days; but they live in such alarms, or greater, from the beginning to the end of the year. I hope, therefore you will be thankful to God, if he is pleased to sheath the sword of war, and to put a stop to the devastations and the slaughters which have so long prevailed. Though you yourself have not been a sufferer, I wish you to cultivate a feeling and benevolent spirit, a disposition to compassionate, if you cannot relieve, the distresses of others. This, next to the grace of God, is the brightest ornament of human nature; or rather when genuine, it is one of the best effects and proofs of grace. It was the mind of Jesus the Savior: They who love him will in a degree resemble him, and they only. A hard-hearted, unfeeling, selfish Christian, is a contradiction.

When you think what multitudes of mankind are suffering by war, famine, sickness, storms, earthquakes, and other calamities, let it lead your thoughts to the evil of sin, which brought all other evils into the world. But what is sin? I endeavored to tell you last Sabbath, from Jer. 2:11. "Hath a nation changed their gods which are yet no gods? But my people have changed their glory for that which doth not profit." Sin is, presuming to do our own will in opposition to the will of God, who is our Creator, Lawgiver, and Benefactor. By sin we affect independence of our Creator, affront the authority of our righteous Lawgiver, and are guilty of base and horrid ingratitude against our greatest and kindest Benefactor.

If you could form a little creature and make it live, if it hated you and opposed you, slighted your kindness, and took a pleasure in displeasing you, would you not soon be weary of it, and, instead of feeding and taking care of it, be provoked to tread it under your feet? But, O the patience of God! Though he could destroy rebellious men much more easily than you can kill a spider or a beetle, yet he waits to be gracious, and has so loved them as to send his own Son to die, that they may live. Sin has not only filled the world with woe, but it was the cause of all the wo that Jesus endured. He groaned, and wept, and sweat blood, and died upon the cross, only because we had sinned. May I live to see you duly affected with the evil of sin, and the love of Jesus; and what more can I ask for?

I am, my dear child,
Your most affectionate father.

Letter 14

March 8, 1783.

My Dear Child,

It would please me if I could either visit you or write to you, or both, every week. But it cannot be; I am behindhand with every body. Yet I think I send you six letters for one. You stare at that; but if you please to count the lines in one of your epistles, and the letters in every line, and then compare it with one of mine, you will find that you receive many more words and letters than you return.

You sometimes intimate that you are afraid of death, and I wonder not at it, for you are a sinner; but I hope to see you a believer, and then you will not greatly fear it, while it is at a distance; and whenever it comes very near, you will not fear it at all. Mr. **** is gone, and so is Mr. ****, and neither of them was more afraid of death than you would be afraid of a coach that should stop at the gate to take you home to us. Jesus died to make death safe and comfortable to us. Balaam was not a good man, but he spoke well when he said, "Let me die the death of the righteous." Make that prayer for yourself; it is a good one, though short. Entreat the Lord to number you among the righteous, that you may live their life; then your death will be like theirs.

The Scripture in many places speaks of the righteous and the wicked, as two characters which divide and comprehend all mankind; and yet it tells us that there is none righteous, no, not one—that is, there are none righteous by nature: Sinners are made righteous by the grace of God. The grace of God teaches them to understand what they read of a Savior, and their own need of a Savior. When they put their trust in him their sins are forgiven them for his sake; and when they rightly consider his love to them, his dying for their sakes, they learn to love him, and they who love him must and will hate what is evil: they learn to resemble him, and study to please him; and thus they are not only accepted as righteous in the Beloved, but they are really made so; the love of righteousness is implanted in their hearts; they believe what the Lord says, they heartily strive to obey his commands, to avoid what he forbids; they place their happiness in his favor, and in doing his will. They cannot but speak of their Savior, and what he has done for them; they love to hear others speak of him, and they love to hear those ministers who preach and talk concerning him;

but their religion does not at all consist in talking and hearing; they are upright, gentle and loving; they imitate him who went about doing good. The evil tempers of self-will, impatience, pride, envy, anger, and malice are put away; they cannot allow themselves to indulge in such passions: If they feel the rising of such things in their hearts, they are grieved and ashamed, and are glad to fly to the Throne of Grace for mercy and help against them. On the other hand, they no longer seek pleasure in the vanities and follies of the world; they have better things to mind. These trifles they lay aside; as we forsake, when we grow up, the playthings which pleased us while we were children.

But you must not expect all this at once. Look at a great tree; an oak for instance; how tall it is! How wide its branches spread! And if you were to dig, you would find it has deep and wide-spreading roots in proportion! Yet this great tree sprang from a little acorn; but not, like a mushroom, in a single night: it has been years in growing, and had you watched it every day you would hardly have perceived that it grew at all. May I not hope that there is at least a little seed of gracious desire already put in your heart? If so, may the Lord, who alone could plant it, water it with his blessing, and cause it to increase; if not, it is my daily prayer that it may be so; and I hope it is your prayer for yourself. I pray that you may live and die with the righteous: It is said of them, they have hope in their death; and that when they see it approach, they say, "O death, where is thy sting?"

Your mamma and I love you dearly, and hope we shall always have reason to love you more and more.

I am your affectionate.

Letter 15

May 12, 1783.

My Dear Child,

I have just now received my child's short and sweet letter; and having nothing to prevent me, I begin my answer to it immediately.

The snow does not often cover the ground in the neighborhood of London so late as the 8th of May; but it has been so sometimes. One reason you were surprised at the sight is, because you are young, and this is the first instance, perhaps, that has occurred in the few years since you began to take notice of such things. You will meet with many other things as you grow up, which will surprise you for the like reason; for want of experience, you will not expect them. We expect flowers on the ground in May, and not snow: So those pleasures, the prospects of which present themselves to your mind and appear at a distance as beautiful as we usually conceive a May morning to be, when we talk of it in winter, will not always answer expectation. When the time comes, something which you did not think of, unseasonable as snow in May, will come with it, and you will be surprised and disappointed; especially at first, and till you are used to these changes. By the time you are as old as I am now, you will not wonder so much; and, I hope, long before that, the Lord will teach you to profit by such things. It is necessary we should find all to be uncertain and unsatisfying in the present world, or we should be contented with it, and not think of a better. One reason why young people are but seldom serious is, because the world appears so pleasing and so promising. They expect roses without thorns, and May without snow. The Lord make you wise betimes, that you may remember and seek him now in the days of your youth, before the evil days come, (for come they will) when you will find no pleasure in them.

Such days are come very early to Miss B****. I wish it were practicable that all the misses in all the schools in London could see her. What are the pleasure and gayety which most are thinking of, now to her—shut up, as she is, in the bloom of life, unable to move herself, and with pain her constant companion day and night? I have been much affected with looking at her; but I believe I shall not see her long. Within these three days she has been much worse. I was with her twice yesterday; and I have been with her again this morning. The doctors think she cannot live many days; and she thinks so too. I am glad to find that she is not unwilling to die. If her affliction has been sanctified to lead her heart to the Lord, then, instead of greatly pitying her, we shall rejoice in her behalf. It is better to be sick or lame, or full of pain, and seeking after him, than to live what is commonly deemed a happy life, without God in the world.

Cannot you contrive to put your lines a little closer together? Your paper looks like a half-furnished room. I want a good long letter; I care not what it is about, so that you write easily. You read sometimes; cannot you find something in your books to tell me of? You walk sometimes, and without doubt look about you. Take notice of any thing that strikes your eye; make some reflection or observation upon it, and then put up your thoughts very safely in a corner of your memory, that you may send them to me the next time you write. I love a long letter, especially from you, because I love you a great deal.

Adieu, the Lord bless you
is the prayer of
Your affectionate.

Letter 16

May 19, 1783.

My Dear Child,

If your sensibility drops a tear or two when you are informed that your aunt C**** is removed from this world of sin and sorrow, I have no objection; but I do not wish you to shed many, nor is there just cause for it. If we could see her now, she would surely say, "Weep not for me, I am happy!" Yes, she knew and loved the Lord; she lived in his faith and fear, and died in his peace and favor; and now she is before the throne. She had her share of trials in this life, but they are all over now: She fought the good fight, and the Lord made her more than conqueror. Now she has received the conqueror's crown, and is singing the conqueror's song.

Methinks, dearly as I love you, I could bear to part with you likewise, if I was sure that the Lord had set his seal of love upon your heart, and thereby marked you for his own. If he has not done this already, I hope he will. If he has not yet taken full possession of your heart, I hope you are sensible that he is standing, as it were, at the door, and knocking, waiting to be gracious to you. The door of the heart is not easily opened. The love of sin, of self, and the world, are so many bolts, which are too strong for us to remove by our own power; yet he can open it easily, (because all things are easy to him,) and, by a sweet constraint of love, force himself an entrance. I hope you are willing that he should do this; and that you are not willing to do anything on your part that may grieve him, and cause him to withdraw and leave you to yourself. You can indeed do nothing spiritually of yourself. Yet there is something for you to do; you are to pray and long for his blessing; you are to read his word, and to endeavor to make it the rule of your conduct, so far as you understand it; you are to attend to his voice in your conscience, and not wilfully allow yourself in what you know to be wrong; you are to repent of your sins and believe in Christ. This is the path in which my heart's desire and prayer is that you may walk; and in due time the promise shall be fulfilled to you which says, "Then shall you know, if you follow on to know the Lord." Hosea, 6:3.

You may believe we had some weeping at home upon this occasion. But the Lord is very good. Your mamma has been supported, and is pretty well.

I long to see you, and especially now, that we may read Mr. Gray's Elegy together. I hope we shall be permitted to be with you on the famous exhibition day, and I please myself with the thought that you will appear to advantage. I wish, for your own sake, you could get the better of that trepidation and hurry which discomposes you when the eyes of company are upon you; but it is a fault on the right side, and much better than a bold, pert, self-confident carriage, which is very disgusting in some young people; but there is a medium which I wish you to aim at.

I am your affectionate.

Letter 17

June 11, 1783.

My Dear Child,

I thank you for your last letter, which pleased me and your mamma very much. We thought it well written and well expressed. Take as much care as you please how you write, and use as little study as you please what to write. When you are surrounded with the beauties of nature, you need not puzzle yourself with thinking what to say first; but set down first what first occurs to your mind; when you have written that, something else will offer. Try to write just what you think, and write as often and as largely as your many important businesses will allow; for nothing but practice will give you a habit of writing easily; and practice will do it. We could fill up as large a sheet as you, with repeating how much we love you: I hope and believe there is no love lost on either side. Love will make you desirous to please and oblige us, and love will prompt us to do everything in our power to oblige and please you; and so I hope we shall go on loving and pleasing as long as we live.

We often think of Monday se'nnight, when we hope to come and see your exhibition. I promise myself that your part will do you credit, and give us satisfaction. I should like to come over and read the Elegy with you once more; but I know I shall not be able, and I believe it will not be necessary. I doubt not but you will do it very well, especially if you can get the better of your diffidence and trepidation. But I had much rather see you a little timid, than see you assuming and affected, as some young people are. I could wish you to have just so much feeling when you begin as might intimate a respect for the company; and then that you should enter into the spirit of the poem, so as in a manner to forget every body present, till you have done. There is a great beauty in the cadence and melody of the verse, if you can hit it off without overdoing it. If you understand and can feel the subject, you will express it properly.

I hope the Elegy will likewise lead you to some profitable reflections for your own use, and which may excite your thankfulness to the Lord. To him you owe your capacity, and to him likewise you are indebted for the advantages you have of cultivation. It is possible, that among the children we meet half naked in the streets, there may be some who might have been amiable and admired in life, if they had been favored with the helps which the good Providence of God has afforded you. But they grow up, poor things, in ignorance and wickedness, after the example of those among whom they live. And though you would not have been like these, yet it is probable you would not have been, as you now may, and I hope will be, if the Lord had not sent you to us. Though you were deprived of your own parents when you were very young, perhaps no child, in such a case has had less cause to feel the loss; because the Lord not only made us willing to take care of you, but gave us, immediately on our receiving you, a tender affection for you, as if you had been our own; and from that time your welfare has been a principal object with us. You have been guarded against the follies and vanities which might otherwise have taken an early possession of your mind; and you have been acquainted with the means of grace and the blessed Gospel. I trust the Lord has a gracious design to lead you to himself, by all these favorable circumstances in which he has placed you; for without this, every thing you can learn or attain would be but of little worth. I wish, indeed, to see you possessed of every accomplishment you can acquire at school; but nothing will satisfy me for you but the grace of God.

I am your very affectionate.

Letter 18

July 29, 1783.

My Dear great Girl,

You seem to take it for granted that I must always write first; and you see I very readily submit, in hopes that when your many important businesses will permit, you will at least oblige me with an answer; for it will give your mamma and me, and your cousin, pleasure to know that you are well.

While you were a little girl, we used, when you came home from N****, to place you with your back against the wall, by the fireplace in the parlor, and compare you with your former marks, that we might notice how much taller you grew from one half year to another. According to present appearances, you are likely to be sufficiently tall and shoot up apace. I need not measure, for I can perceive, by a glance of the eye, that you are grown every time you return to us. But I am watching your growth in another sense with more attention—I wish I could say with more satisfaction. I wish to see you outgrow a certain childishness, which once looked very pretty in you, but is by no means so pleasing in a person of your years, and of your size; I think I may add, of your sense too, for I know the Lord has given you a good measure of understanding and natural abilities; so that with a proper degree of attention and application, you are capable of every attainment suitable to your sex and your situation in life. I love to call you my dear child, and shall probably call you so as long as I live, because there is something to me in the sound of the word *child*, expressive of the tenderness and affection I feel for you; but I would not always have you a child in the common sense of the word. I hope you will not think that I am angry with you, and I hope you will not be angry with me for giving you this hint. I love to see you cheerful, but then I would have you remember that it is high time that a measure of thought, and steadiness, and attention should begin to mark your general deportment.

Your dear mamma, at your age, was capable of superintending the affairs of the family, and was actually called to it; and you are now old enough, if you will do yourself justice, to take a great deal of care off from her hands when you are at home; you have it in your own power to shorten the term of your living away from us. I am glad that though you like your school very well, yet you like home better; and I am sure we shall be glad when we can think it no longer necessary to keep you abroad, for we love your company, and it is principally for your own sake that we are constrained to part with you. But they say, a word to the wise is enough, and therefore I shall add no more in this strain.

You heard several of my sermons on Mary and Martha. Last Sabbath night I finished the subject by speaking on, "One thing is needful"—a sentence which I pray the Lord to write upon your heart. Many things are necessary in their places; but one thing is absolutely needful. It is right that you should be diligent at school, obedient and obliging to your governess and teachers, and that you should endeavor, by a kind and gentle behavior, to gain the esteem of your school-fellows and of the whole family: A regard to the one thing needful is very consistent with all this. But though you were beloved by every body that knows you, you cannot be happy except you know and love the Lord. The one thing needful, therefore, is to seek him, and his favor, which is better than life; and if you seek him, he will be found of you.

You are a sinner and need forgiveness; you have wants which he only can supply; you are growing up in a world which is full of sins, snares, troubles, and dangers. Will you not cry to him then, "My Father, thou art the guide of my youth!" You have encouragement to seek him, for he himself both invites and commands you to do it; and if obligations and gratitude can prevail, there is no friend like him, whose mercies are new every morning, and who died upon the cross to redeem us from misery. I commend you to his blessing.

Your cousin is much as she was; she sends her love to you. I believe she loves you dearly, and I believe you love her. I hope you will both love each other as long as you live upon this earth; and that afterwards you will meet in the kingdom of love, and be happy together in heaven for ever. Mamma sends her best love. Believe me to be often thinking of you, and praying for you, and always desirous to show my love in deed and in truth.

Your affectionate.

Letter 19

October 16, 1783.

My Dear Child,

I hope you will not be able to rest yourself; for you have had a sad hurrying time since Midsummer. So much visiting and running about has, I hope, given you a right relish for the retirement and regularity of school. What a pretty place you are in, and what a pretty time of life it is with you, if you can but think so, before trouble and care have received commission to disturb you.

I could wish that all my letters might afford you both pleasure and profit; I would make you smile sometimes, and always endeavor to do you good. At present I must write a little upon the subject of temper. I do not think your temper a bad one. Your mamma and I are always ready to give you a good character, and it pleases us that we can say you are, in the main, affectionate and obliging. But we sometimes observe that in you which we could wish nobody took notice of but ourselves; or rather, that you would strive to get quite the better of it, that we who love you so dearly might be no more grieved. It is a certain self-willed impatience, which disposes you, when your inclinations are overruled, or when any thing is desired of you which does not exactly please you, to pout, frown, and alter your countenance, so that you often appear to disadvantage in company. You do not seem to find, or think of finding, a pleasure in giving up a thing to please your mamma, but had rather have your own way. Now if you sit down and consider how much we love you, and study to oblige and please you, I hope you will strive against this irritable temper: I do not believe it is owing to a want of affection and gratitude on your part, but rather the effect of a something in your natural temper, which, if you strive against, I hope you will be enabled to overcome.

Besides what you owe to our love and tenderness, I can give you a further reason why you should attend to this point. I have told you repeatedly, and I tell you again, that your cousin's coming to live with us will not make the slightest alteration in our love for you. You are still and will be our own dear child; we have love enough for you both. But in the outward expression of our love, something must of course depend upon behavior. We are sometimes obliged, though with reluctance, to reprove and contradict you; now we cannot reprove her because she never gives us an opportunity. In the seven months she has been with us, I never once knew her debate with us, nor have I once seen a cloud upon her brow for a single moment. She watches our looks, and if she perceives the slightest hint that any thing she proposes is not quite agreeable to us, she has done with it in a moment, and gives it up with a smile; which shows that it costs her nothing, but that she really prefers pleasing us to pleasing herself. Now you must allow, my dear, that this behavior is very engaging. I wish you to be equally engaging; and not to seem to come short of her in any thing.

Have you heard of your good friend Mrs. ****'s illness? They have no expectation of her recovery; nay, perhaps she is dead before this time. How well she seemed when we dined there but lately! So uncertain is life—even young people have no assurance of continuing here; but I hope you will pray as David did, "Lord, make me to know mine end, and the measure of my days, what it is; that I may know how frail I am," Psalm 39:4, and that the Lord will hear your prayer. When you come to know him as your Lord and Savior, you may sing Simeon's song. And we cannot enjoy life with true comfort till we are delivered from the fear of death.

I am your affectionate.

Letter 20

October 23, 1783.

My Dear Child,

When I showed my last letter to your mamma, I thought she looked as if she was almost unwilling I should send it; but she did not say so, and therefore it went. She is unwilling to give you pain, and so am I. But I persuaded myself you would take it (as I meant it) as a proof of my love. Now and then I must gently give you a word of advice, but it will always be much more pleasing to me to commend than to find fault. Your welfare is very near my heart, and I feel a warm desire that your behavior in every respect should be such as to engage the esteem and affection of all who know you. I remember, when you were a little girl at Northampton school, I once told you in a letter, that when the Lord in his providence sent you to my care I received you as his gift; and in the pleasing hope of being an instrument in his hand of doing you good, I found such affection for you that I would not part with you for your weight in gold. And though you are much heavier now than you were then, I can say the same still.

Mrs. W**** had been ill some days before I heard of it, and then I was told she was at the point of death. This information, with some hinderances and difficulties in the way, prevented my going to—; so that I did not see her. She was an old and kind acquaintance, and though of late years I was not often in her company, I feel that I have lost a friend whom I loved. Such is the state of this world. If we live long in it, we must expect to see our friends drop off, one after another, as the leaves at this season of the year fall from the trees. But the pain which Christians feel at parting with their Christian friends is alleviated by two considerations; first that, now they are gone they are much more happy than they could be here; and secondly, we hope ere long to be with them again, and to share in their songs and joys before the throne of God. This, my dear child, is the desire of my soul for you, that while you live, and when you die, you may be the Lord's. Nothing but this will satisfy me. And for this I often pray.

My thoughts and prayers are often employed for you when perhaps you are asleep. I cannot make many very particular requests for you, because I know not what is best for you; but when I pray that you may have wisdom and grace to seek and know the Lord, and that he will be graciously pleased to be your Savior and Shepherd, and the guide of your youth, I am sure I do not ask amiss. I have a cheerful hope that he will put you among his children, guide you through this wilderness world by his counsel, and afterwards receive you to his glory; and that he sent you to me, that you might have the benefit of those means of grace and instruction which, by his blessing, will be effectual to make you wise unto salvation.

Though he alone can work in you to will and to do according to his good pleasure, yet there is something incumbent on you. He has said, "They who seek me shall find me." You must therefore seek him; and he is not far from you. He is about your bed and about your path. Yea, he is still nearer. I hope there are seasons when you can perceive him knocking, as it were, at the door of your heart. Do not you at times perceive something within you bearing witness to the truths of his word; warning you of the evil of sin, reminding you of death and eternity, and stirring up your desires towards himself? At such times you may be sure the Lord is near. He made the heart, and he knows how to affect it.

Such warnings and calls from his good Spirit I can recollect when I was a child younger than you. I can remember getting into corners by myself, and praying with earnestness, before I was eight years old. Afterwards, alas! I proved rebellious. I cast off his fear, and would have my own way; and thereby I plunged myself into abundance of sin and misery. But I hope you will be more obedient. Think of him as often as you can; make a point of praying to him in secret, remembering that when you are most alone, he is still with you. When you pray, endeavor simply to express your wants and feelings just as if you were speaking to me. Fine words and phrases some people abound in; but true prayer is the genuine language of the heart, which the Lord understands and accepts, however brokenly expressed. The woman of Canaan only said, "Lord, help me!" The publican's prayer was almost as short, "God be merciful to me a sinner!" and both were heard.

The Bible, or the New Testament, is frequently used at school as a school-book; and children often think no more of it than just to read their appointed lesson. But I hope you will consider it as God's book, and when you take it in hand, open it with reverence, and read it with attention, as you think you would if you expected to hear him speak to you with an audible voice from heaven. The plainest and most affecting part of the Bible is the history of our Savior in the Evangelists; read it often, that you may be well acquainted with it. I pray him to enable you to understand what you read. Surely when you read who he is, what he did, what he suffered, and what he has promised to poor sinners, you will, you must love him! And if you once love him, you will study to please him. The Lord bless you. Give our love to your governess, and all friends.

Believe me to be your very affectionate.

Letter 21

October 30, 1783.

My Dear Child,

Though I lately sent you a long letter by the post, which I hope you received on Tuesday, I must write again; and I take a new pen and a sheet of gilt paper, that I may, in the best manner I can, make you a return for your letter which I received yesterday. I would not delay long to let you know how much your mamma and I were pleased with it. It is a great happiness to us that we are well assured of your desire and intention to oblige us; and we hope not to be behindhand with you.

We are very far from thinking your temper is bad; the manner of your answer is a proof of the contrary. You may sometimes need a word of advice or admonition; I believe even this will not be often necessary; and when there is occasion, my affection will prompt me to offer it with so much tenderness, that it shall look as little like reproof as possible: and I hope and expect to find many more occasions for commending than for reproving you.

Should it please the Lord to spare your cousin, a time will come when you will live together, and, I believe, love each other dearly. I would certainly wish you to imitate her in any thing that you see is commendable; and there will be other things, I trust, in which you may be a pattern to her. Thus you may be mutually useful to each other; and we will love you both, and rejoice in you both. We shall not love you a hair's breadth the less than we should have done if we had never seen her.

Indeed I cannot be sufficiently thankful to the Lord, that when he was pleased in his Providence to put two children under my care, they should both be of such amiable, affectionate dispositions, as would win my love if they had been strangers, and not so nearly related as you and your cousin are to us. And though I consider you both now as my own children, yet you are still my eldest, and my having a second will be no prejudice to your birthright.

I have not a bit of news that I can think of to send you. Your mamma is pretty well, and your cousin likewise; but she is much confined, for if the weather is either wet or cold, we cannot venture her abroad. She does not seem to want to go out, except to church. When we are going thither, it is some trial to her to be left behind; but she is satisfied, because she thinks her aunt is the most proper judge whether she can go with safety or not.

You, my dear, are favored with health, and I hope you will be thankful for it. Your cousin, and twenty other young people I could name, know the value of health by the want of it. The Lord can make sickness a blessing when he is pleased to send it; but still a good state of health is a great privilege. If your life should be prolonged, it may be a good while before increase of years makes a sensible change in your constitution, but you will feel it at last. When you see an old woman tottering about with a stick, consider that she was once as young as you are now, and probably her spirits as lively and her limbs as agile as yours. Suppose it may be fifty years before you are like her, such a space which seems long beforehand, will seem very short when it is past, and there is hardly one in fifty of your age that will be alive fifty years hence.

Dangers stand thick through all the ground,
To push us to our tomb;
And fierce diseases wait around,
To hurry mortals home.

How just, therefore, and important is that advice, "Remember thy Creator in the days of thy youth, before the evil days come."

And whom should we remember, if we forget him? Our Creator is our Redeemer. Isa. 54:5; the Savior, the Lover of souls, who assumed our nature that he might be capable of dying for us. Shall we not remember him who endured agonies, and sweat blood, and hung upon the cross, that we might escape the misery we deserved, and be made the children of God? I wish the poet's words may express the very feeling of your heart and mine!—

Remember thee!—

Yes, from the table of my memory
I'll wipe away all trivial fond records,
All saws of books, all forms, all pressures past,
That youth and observation copied there;
And thy commandment all alone shall live
Within the book and volume of my brain,
Unmix'd with baser matter.

I commend you to his love, and pray him to write his name upon your heart. We all join in love to you.

Believe me to be your affectionate

THE END

Eliza Cunningham

by Rev. John Newton
Rector of St. Mary Woolnoth, London.

When the following narrative was drawn up, the writer was aware that his feelings rendered him incompetent to judge how much of a relation, every part of which was interesting to himself, might be fit to offer to the public. He therefore wrote only for his friends, and printed no more copies than would be sufficient to distribute within the circle of his personal acquaintance. But as the paper has been much inquired after, and many of his friends have expressed a wish that it might be more extensively circulated, he has at length yielded to their judgment.

It is to be lamented that, in this enlightened age, religion should, by many, be thought the only subject unworthy of a serious inquiry. And that while, in every branch of science, they are cautious of admitting any theory which cannot stand the test of experiment, they treat the use of the term Experimental, when applied to religion, with contempt. Yet there are many things connected with this subject, in which, whether we are willing or unwilling, we are and must be nearly interested. Death, for instance, is inevitable; and the consequences of death must be important. Many persons die, as they live, thoughtless of what consequences may await them. Others leave the world with reluctance and terror. And there are others who, though conscious that they are sinners, and sure that they are about to enter on an unchangeable and endless state of existence, possess peace, composure, and joy. These declare, that they owe this happy state of mind to their dependence on Jesus the Saviour, on whose death and mediation they have built their hopes. And who can disprove their words? Such an instance is now in the reader's hands. The fact is indubitable. A child, under the age of fifteen, did thus rejoice in the midst of pains and agonies, to the admiration of all who beheld her. She was willing to leave all her friends whom she dearly loved, and by whom she was tenderly beloved; for she knew whom she believed, and that when she should be absent from the body, she should be present with the Lord. With this assurance, she triumphed in the prospect of glory, and smiled upon the approach of death.

Narrative, Etc

As I write, not for the eye of the public, but chiefly to put a testimony of the Lord's goodness into the hands of my dear friends, who have kindly afforded us their sympathy and prayers on the late occasion, I do not mean either to restrain the emotions of my heart, or to apologize for them. I shall write simply and freely, as I might speak to a person to whose intimacy and tenderness I might fully entrust myself, and who, I know, will bear with all my weaknesses.

In May, 1782, my sister Cunningham was at Edinburgh, chiefly on the account of her eldest daughter, then in the 14th year of her age, who was very ill of a consumption. She had already buried an only son, at the age of twelve; and while all a mother's care and feelings were engaged by the rapid decline of a second amiable child, she was unexpectedly bereaved of an affectionate and excellent husband. Her trials were great; but the Lord had prepared her for them. She was a believer. Her faith was strong, her graces active, her conduct exemplary. She walked with God, and he supported her. And though she was a tender and sympathizing friend, she had a happy firmness of temper; so that her character, as a Christian, and the propriety of her behavior in every branch of relative life, appeared with peculiar advantage in the season of affliction. She returned to Anstruther a widow, with her sick child, who languished till October, and then died.

Though my sister had many valuable and pleasing connections in Scotland, yet her strongest tie being broken, she readily accepted my invitation to come and live with us. She was not only dear to me as Mrs. Newton's sister, but we had lived long in the habits of intimate friendship. I knew her worth, and she was partial to me. She had yet one child remaining, her dear Eliza. We already had a dear orphan niece, whom we had, about seven years before, adopted for our own daughter. My active, fond, imagination anticipated the time of her arrival, and drew a pleasing picture of the addition the company of such a sister, such a friend, would make to the happiness of our family. The children likewise—there was no great disparity between them either in years or stature. From what I had heard of Eliza, I was prepared to love her before I saw her; though she came afterwards into my hands like a heap of untold gold, which, when counted over, proves to be a larger sum than was expected. My fancy paired and united these children; I hoped that the friendship between us and my sister would be perpetuated in them. I seemed to see them, like twin sisters, of one heart and mind, habited nearly alike, always together, always with us.

Such was my plan; but the Lord's plan was very different, and therefore mine failed. It is happy for us, poor short-sighted mortals, unable as we are to foresee the consequences of our own wishes, that if we know and trust him, he often is pleased to put a merciful negative upon our purposes, and condescends to choose better for us than we can for ourselves. What might have been the issue of my plan, had it taken place, I know not; but I can now praise and adore him for the gracious issue of his. I praise his name, that I can cheerfully comply with his word, which says, "Be still, and know that I am God." I not only can bow, as it becomes a creature and a sinner to do, to his sovereignty, but I admire his wisdom and goodness, and can say from my heart, "He has done all things well."

My sister had settled her affairs previous to her removal; and nothing remained but to take leave of her friends, of whom she had many, not only in Anstruther, but in different parts of the country. In February, 1783, I received a letter from her, which, before I opened it, I expected was to inform me that she was upon the road in her way to London. But the information was, that, in a little journey she had made to bid a friend farewell, she had caught a violent cold, which brought on a fever and a cough, with other symptoms, which, although she described as gently as possible, that we might not be alarmed, obliged *me* to give up instantly the hope of seeing her.

Succeeding letters confirmed my suspicions; her malady increased, and she was soon confined to her bed.

Eliza was at school at Musselburgh. Till then she had enjoyed a perfect state of health; but while her dear mother was rapidly declining, *she* likewise caught a great cold, and her life likewise was soon thought to be in danger. On this occasion, that fortitude and resolution which strongly marked my sister's character, was remarkably displayed. She knew that her own race was almost finished; she earnestly desired that Eliza might live or die with us; and the physicians advised a speedy removal into the south. Accordingly, to save time, and to save Eliza from the impression which the sight of a dying mother might probably make upon her spirits, and possibly apprehensive that the interview might make too great an impression upon her own, she sent this, her only, beloved child, directly to London, without letting her come home to take a last leave of her. She contented herself with committing and bequeathing her child to our care and love, in a letter, which, I believe, was the last she was able to write.

Thus powerfully recommended by the pathetic charge of a dying mother, the dearest friend we had upon earth, and by that plea for compassion which her illness might have strongly urged even upon strangers, we received our dear Eliza, as a trust, and as a treasure, on the 15th of March. My sister lived long enough to have the comfort of knowing, not only that she was safely arrived, but was perfectly pleased with her new situation. She was now freed from all earthly cares. She suffered much in the remaining part of her illness, but she knew whom she believed; she possessed a peace past understanding, and a hope full of glory. She entered into the joy of her Lord on the 10th of May, 1783, respected and regretted by all who knew her.

I soon perceived that the Lord had sent me a treasure indeed. Eliza's person was agreeable. There was an ease and elegance in her whole address, and a gracefulness in her movements, till long illness and great weakness bowed her down. Her disposition was lively, her genius quick and inventive; and if she had enjoyed health, she probably would have excelled in every thing that required ingenuity. Her understanding, particularly her judgment and her sense of propriety, were far above her years. There was something in her appearance that usually procured her favor at the first sight. She was honored by the notice of several persons of distinction, which, though I thankfully attribute in part to their kindness to me, I believe was a good deal owing to something rather uncommon in her.

But her principal endearing qualities, which could be only fully known to us who lived with her, were the sweetness of her temper, and a heart formed for the exercise of affection, gratitude, and friendship. Whether, when at school, she might have heard sorrowful tales from children, who, having lost their parents, met with a great difference in point of tenderness when they came under the direction of uncles and aunts, and might think that all uncles and aunts were alike, I know not; but I have understood since from herself, that she did not come to us with any highly-raised expectations of the treatment she was to meet with.

But as she found, (the Lord in mercy having opened our hearts to receive her,) that it was hardly possible for her own parents to have treated her more tenderly, and that it was from that time the business and the pleasure of our lives to study how to oblige her, and how to alleviate the afflictions which we were unable to remove; so we likewise found, that the seeds of our kindness could hardly be sown in a more promising and fruitful soil. I know not that either her aunt or I ever saw a cloud upon her countenance during the time she was with us. It is true, we did not, we could not, unnecessarily cross her; but if we thought it expedient to overrule any proposal she made, she acquiesced with a sweet smile; and we were certain we should never hear of that proposal again. Her delicacy, however, was quicker than our observation; and she would sometimes say, when we could not perceive the least reason for it, "I am afraid I answer you peevishly; indeed I did not intend it; if I did, I ask your pardon; I should be very ungrateful if I thought any pleasure equal to that of endeavoring to please you." It is no wonder that we dearly loved such a child.

The hectic fever, cough, and sweats, which she brought with her from Scotland, were subdued in the course of the summer, and there appeared no reason to apprehend that she would be taken off very suddenly. But still there was a worm preying upon the root of this pretty gourd. She had seldom any severe pain till within the last fortnight of her life, and usually slept well; but when awake she was always ill. I believe she knew not a single hour of perfect ease; and they who intimately knew her state, could not but wonder to see her so placid, cheerful, and attentive, when in company as she generally was. Many a time, when the tears have silently stolen down her cheeks, if she saw that her aunt or I observed her, she would wipe them away, come to us with a smile and a kiss, and say, "Do not be uneasy—I am not very ill—I can bear it—I shall be better presently;" or to that effect.

In April, 1784, we put her under the care of my dear friend, Dr. Benamor. To the blessing of the Lord on his skill and endeavors, I ascribe the pleasure of having her continued with us so long; nor can I sufficiently express my gratitude for his assiduous, unwearied attention, nor for his great tenderness. She is now gone, and can no more repeat, what she has often spoken, of the great comfort it was to her to have so affectionate and sympathizing a physician; but while I live, I hope it will always be my pleasure to acknowledge our great obligations to him on her account. His prescriptions were carefully followed. But what can the most efficacious medicines or the best physicians avail to prolong life, when the hour approaches, in which the prayer of the great Intercessor must be accomplished, "Father, I will that they whom thou hast given me may be with me where I am, to behold my glory!" This was the proper cause of my dear Eliza's death. The Lord sent this child to me to be brought up for him; he owned my poor endeavors; and when her education was completed, and she was ripened for heaven, he took her home to himself. He has richly paid me my wages, in the employment itself, and in the happy issue.

I have thus put together, in one view, a brief account of what relates to her illness, till within the last three weeks of her pilgrimage. I now come to what is much more important and interesting. Her excellent parents had conscientiously endeavored to bring her up in the nurture and admonition of the Lord, and principles of religion were instilled into her from infancy. Their labors were so far successful, that no child could be more obedient or obliging, or more remote from evil habits or evil tempers. But I could not perceive, when she first came to us, that she had any heart-affecting sense of divine things; but being under my roof, she, of course, when her health would permit, attended on my ministry, and was usually present when I prayed and expounded the Scriptures, morning and evening in the family. Friends and ministers were likewise frequently with us, whose character and conversation were well suited to engage her notice, and to help her to form a right idea of the Christian principles and temper.

Knowing that she was of a thinking turn, I left her to make her own reflections upon what she saw and heard, committing her to the direction of the Lord, from whom I had received her, and entreating him to be her effectual teacher. When I did attempt to talk with her on the concerns of her soul, she could give me no answer but with tears. But I soon had great encouragement to hope that the Lord had both enlightened her understanding, and had drawn the desires of her heart to himself. Great was her delight in the ordinances; exemplary her attention under the preaching. To be debarred from going to hear at our stated times was a trial, which, though she patiently bore, seemed to affect her more than any other; and she did not greatly care what she endured in the rest of the week, provided she was well enough to attend the public worship. The judicious observations she occasionally made upon what had passed in conversation, upon incidents, books, and sermons, indicated a sound, scriptural judgment, and a spiritual taste. And my hope was confirmed by her whole deportment, which was becoming the Gospel of Christ. So that had she died suddenly on any day within about a year and a half past, I should have had no doubt that she had passed from death unto life. But I could seldom prevail with her to speak of herself; if she did, it was with the greatest diffidence and caution.

In the last two or three weeks of her life, she became acquainted with acute pain, to which she had till then been much a stranger. Her gentle spirit, which had borne up under a long and languishing illness, was not so capable of supporting pain. It did not occasion any improper temper of language, but it wore her away apace. Friday, the 30th of September, she was down stairs for the last time, and then she was brought down and carried up in my arms.

It now became very desirable to hear from herself a more explicit account of the hope that was in her; especially as upon some symptoms of an approaching mortification, she appeared to be a little alarmed, and of course not thoroughly reconciled to the thoughts of death. Her aunt waited for the first convenient opportunity of intimating to her the probability that the time of her departure was at hand. The next morning, Saturday, the first of October, presented one. She found herself remarkably better: Her pains were almost gone; her spirits revived: The favorable change was visible in her countenance.

Her aunt began to break the subject to her, by saying, "My dear, were you not extremely ill last night?"

She answered, "Indeed I was."

"Had you not been relieved, I think you could not have continued long."

"I believe I could not."

"My dear, I have been very anxiously concerned for your life."

"But I hope, my dear aunt, you are not so now."

She then opened her mind, and spoke freely. I cannot repeat the whole. The substance was to this effect.

"My views of things have been, for some time, very different from what they were when I came to you. I have seen and felt the vanity of childhood and youth."

Her aunt said, "I believe you have long made conscience of secret prayer."

She answered, "Yes, I have long and earnestly sought the Lord, with reference to the change that is now approaching. I have not that full assurance which is so desirable; but I have a hope, I trust a good hope; and I believe the Lord will give me whatever he sees necessary for me before he is pleased to take me hence." She then said, "I have prayed to him to fit me for himself; and then, whether it be sooner or later, it signifies but little."

Here was a comfortable point gained. We were satisfied that she had given up all expectations of living, and could speak of her departure without being distressed.

It will not be expected that a child of her age should speak systematically. Nor had she learned her religion from a system or form of words, however sound. The Lord himself was her teacher. But from what little she had at different times said to me, I was well satisfied that she had received a true conviction of the nature of sin, and of her own state by nature as a sinner. When she spoke of the Lord, she meant the Lord Jesus Christ, the great Shepherd, who gathers such lambs in his arms, and carries them in his bosom. She believed him to be God and man in one person; and that hope of which she was not ashamed, was founded on his atonement, grace, and power. As I do not intend to put words into her mouth which she never spoke, I mention this, lest any should be disappointed at not finding a certain phraseology to which they have been accustomed.

Her apparent revival was of short duration. In the evening of the same day, she complained of a sore throat, which became worse, and by Sabbath noon threatened suffocation. When Dr. Benamor, who the day before had almost entertained hopes of her recovery, found her so suddenly and greatly altered, he could not, at the moment, prevent some signs of concern from appearing in his countenance. She quickly perceived it, and desired he would plainly tell her his sentiments.

When he had recovered himself, he said, "My dear, you are not so well as when I saw you on Saturday."

She answered, that she trusted all would be well soon.

He replied, that whether she lived or died it would be well, and to the glory of God. He told me that he had much pleasing conversation with her that morning, some particulars of which he had committed to writing, but that he had lost the paper. From that time she may be said to have been dying, as we expected her departure from one hour to another.

On Monday, October 3rd, she was almost free from any complaint in the throat; but there was again an appearance of a mortification in her legs; it was, however, again repelled by the means which Dr. Benamor prescribed.

I recollect but little of the incidents of this day: In general she was in great pain, sometimes in agonies, unable to remain many minutes in the same position; but her mind was peaceful. She possessed a spirit of recollection and prayer; and her chief attention to earthly things was confined to the concern she saw in those around her. That she might not increase their distress, she strove to conceal the sense of her sufferings. It pleased the Lord wonderfully to support my dear Mrs. Newton, and she had a tolerable night's rest, though I did not expect the child would live till morning.

On Tuesday, the 4th, about nine in the morning, we all thought her dying, and waited nearly two hours by her bedside, for her last breath. She was much convulsed, and in great agonies.

I said, "My dear, you are going to heaven; and I hope, by the grace of God, we shall in due time follow you."

She could not speak, but let us know by a gentle nod of her head, and a sweet smile, that she attended to what I said.

I repeated to her many passages of Scripture and verses of hymns, to each of which she made the same kind of answer. Though silent, her looks were more expressive than words.

Towards eleven o'clock, a great quantity of coagulated phlegm, which she had not strength to bring up, made her rattle violently in the throat, which we considered as a sign that death was at hand; and as she seemed unwilling to take something that was offered to her, we were loath to disturb her in her last moments, (as we supposed,) by pressing her. I think she must have died in a quarter of an hour, had not Dr. Benamor just then come into the room.

He felt her pulse, and observed that she was not near death by her pulse, and desired that something might be given her. She was perfectly sensible, though still unable to speak, but expressed her unwillingness to take any thing, by her strongest efforts. However, she yielded to entreaty, and a teaspoonful or two of some liquid soon cleared the passage, and she revived. Her pain, however, was extreme, and her disappointment great. I never saw her so near impatience as on this occasion. As soon as she could speak, she cried, "O cruel, cruel, cruel, to recall me, when I was so happy, and so near gone! I wish you had not come—I long to go home." But in a few minutes she grew composed, assented to what the doctor said of her duty to wait the Lord's time; and from that hour, though her desires to depart and to be with her Saviour were stronger and stronger, she cheerfully took whatever was offered to her, and frequently asked for something, of her own accord.

How often, were we to have our choice, should we counteract our own prayers! I had entreated the Lord to prolong her life, till she could leave an indisputable testimony behind her for our comfort: Yet when I saw her agony, and heard her say, O how cruel to stop me! I was for a moment almost of her mind, and could hardly help wishing that the doctor had delayed his visit a little longer. But if she had died then, we should have been deprived of what we saw and heard the two following days; the remembrance of which is now much more precious to me than silver or gold.

When the doctor came on Wednesday, she entreated him to tell her how long he thought she might live.

He said, "Are you in earnest, my dear?"

She answered, "Indeed I am."

At that time there were very great appearances that a mortification was actually begun. He therefore told her, he thought it possible she might hold out till eight in the evening, but did not expect she could survive midnight at farthest. On hearing him say so, low as she was, her eyes seemed to sparkle with their former vivacity; and fixing them on him with an air of ineffable satisfaction, she said, "Oh, that is good news indeed." And she repeated it as such to a person who came soon after into the room, and said, with lively emotions of joy, "The doctor tells me I shall stay here but a few hours longer." In the afternoon she noticed and counted the clock, I believe every time it struck; and when it struck seven, she said, "Another hour, and then." But it pleased the Lord to spare her to us another day.

She suffered much in the course of Wednesday night, but was quite resigned and patient. Our kind servants, who, from their love to her and to us, watched her day and night with a solicitude and tenderness which wealth is too poor to purchase, were the only witnesses of the affectionate and grateful manner in which she repeatedly thanked them for their services and attention to her. Though such an acknowledgement was no more than due, yet coming from herself, and at such a time, they highly valued it. She added her earnest prayers that the Lord would reward them. To her prayers my heart says, Amen. May they be comforted of the Lord in their dying hours, as she was, and meet with equal kindness from those around them!

I was surprised on Thursday morning to find her not only alive, but in some respects better. The tokens of mortification again disappeared. This was her last day, and it was a memorable day with us. When Dr. Benamor asked her how she did,

"Truly happy," said she, "and if this be dying, it is a pleasant thing to die." (The very expression which a dear friend of mine used upon her death-bed a few years ago.)

She said to me, about ten o'clock, "My dear uncle, I would not change conditions with any person upon earth: O, how gracious is the Lord to me! Oh, what a change is before me!" She was several times asked if she could wish to live, provided the Lord would restore her to perfect health; her answer was, "Not for all the world;" and sometimes, "Not for a thousand worlds."

The last time she was asked this question, she said, as I have been since informed, "I desire to have no choice." "Do not weep for me," said she, "my dear aunt, but rather rejoice and praise on my account."

We asked her if she would choose a text for her own funeral sermon.

She readily mentioned, "Whom the Lord loveth he chasteneth." "That," said she, "has been my experience; my afflictions have been many, but not one too many; nor has the greatest of them all been too great; I praise him for them all." But after a pause, she said, "Stay, I think there is another text which may do better; let it be, 'Blessed are the dead which die in the Lord;' THAT is my experience NOW." She likewise chose a hymn to be sung after the sermon.

"In vain my fancy strives to paint
The moment after death;
The glories that surround a saint
When yielding up his breath.

One gentle sigh his fetters breaks,
We scarce can say, 'He's gone!'
Before the willing spirit takes
Its mansion near the throne.

Faith strives, but all its efforts fail,
To trace the spirit's flight;
No eye can pierce within the vail

Which hides the world of light.

Thus much (and this is all) we know,
Saints are completely blest;
Have done with sin, and care, and woe,
And with their Saviour rest:

On harps of gold they praise his name,
His face they always view;
Then let us followers be of them,
That we may praise him too."

But I must check myself, and set down but a small part of the gracious words which the Lord enabled her to speak in the course of the day, though she was frequently interrupted by pains and agonies.

She had something to say, either in a way of admonition or consolation, as she thought most suitable, to every one she saw.

To her most constant attendant she said, "Be sure you continue to call on the Lord; and if you think he does not hear you now, he will at last, as he has heard me."

She spoke a great deal to an intimate friend, who was with her every day, which I hope she will long remember, as the testimony of her dying Eliza. Among other things, she said, "See how comfortable the Lord can make a dying bed! Do you think that you shall have such an assurance when you come to die?"

Being answered, "I hope so, my dear;" she replied,

"But do you earnestly, and with all your heart, pray to the Lord for it? If you seek him, you shall surely find him." She then prayed affectionately and fervently for her friend, afterwards for her cousin, and then for another of our family who was present. Her prayer was not long, but every word was weighty, and her manner was very affecting. The purport was, that they might all be taught and comforted by the Lord.

About five in the afternoon, she desired me to pray with her once more. Surely I then prayed from my heart. When I had finished, she said, "Amen."

I said, "My dear child, have I expressed your meaning?"

She answered, "O, yes!" and then added, "I am ready to say, Why are his chariot wheels so long in coming? But I hope he will enable me to wait his hour with patience."

These were the last words I heard her speak.

Mrs. Newton's heart was much, perhaps too much, attached to this dear child; which is not to be wondered at, considering what sort of a child she was, and how long and how much she had suffered. But the Lord was pleased graciously to support her in this trying season. Indeed, there was more cause for joy than for grief; yet the pain of separation will be felt. Eliza well knew her feelings, and a concern for her was, I believe, the last anxiety that remained with her. She said to those about her, "Try to persuade my aunt to leave the room; I think I shall soon go to sleep; I shall not remain with you till the morning." Her aunt, however, was the last person who heard her speak, and was sitting by her bed when she went away.

A little after six, hearing that a relation who dearly loved her, and was beloved by her, who had come daily from Westminster to see her, was below stairs, she said, "Raise me up, that I may speak to him once more."

Her aunt said, "My dear, you are nearly exhausted, I think you had better not attempt it."

She smiled, and said, "It is very well, I will not."

She was then within half an hour of her translation to glory; but the love of her dear Lord had so filled her with benevolence, that she was ready to exert herself to her last breath, in hope of saying something that might be useful to others after she was gone.

Towards seven o'clock, I was walking in the garden, and earnestly engaged in prayer for her, when a servant came to me and said, "She is gone." O Lord, how great is thy power! How great is thy goodness! A few days before, had it been practicable and lawful, what would I not have given to procure her recovery? Yet seldom in my life have I known a more heartfelt joy than when these words, *She is gone*, sounded in my ears. I ran up stairs, and our whole little family was soon around her bed. Though her aunt and another person were sitting with their eyes fixed upon her, she was gone perhaps a few minutes before she was missed. She lay upon her left side, with her cheek gently reclining upon her hand, as if in a sweet sleep; and I thought there was a smile upon her countenance. Never, surely, did death appear in a more beautiful, inviting form. We fell upon our knees, and I returned, I think I may say, my most unfeigned thanks to our God and Saviour, for his abundant goodness to her, crowned in this last instance, by giving her so gentle a dismission. Yes, I am satisfied; I am comforted. And if one of the many involuntary tears I have shed, could have recalled her to life, to health, to an assemblage of all that this world could contribute to her happiness, I would have labored hard to suppress it. Now my largest desires for her are accomplished. The days of her mourning are ended. She is landed on that peaceful shore where the storms of trouble never blow. She is for ever out of the reach of sorrow, sin, temptation, and snares. Now is she before the throne; she sees him, whom not having seen, she loved; she drinks of the rivers of pleasure which are at his right hand, and shall thirst no more.

She was born February 6, 1771.

She breathed her spirit into her Redeemer's hands a little before seven in the evening, on October 6, 1785, aged fourteen years and eight months.

I shall be glad if this little narrative may prove an encouragement to Christians who have children. May we not conceive the Lord saying to us, as Pharaoh's daughter said to the mother of Moses, "Take this child, and bring it up for me, and I will pay thee thy wages"?

How solemn the trust! Important and difficult the charge of it! But how rich the reward, if our endeavors are crowned with success! And we have every thing to hope from his power and goodness, if, in dependence upon his blessing, we can fully and diligently aim at fulfilling his will. Happy they, who shall say at the last day, "Behold, here am I, and the children which thou hast given me!"

Many children will likewise see this narrative. May it convince them that it is practicable and good to seek the Lord betimes! My dear Eliza's state of languor prevented her from associating with young people of her own age so frequently and freely as she might otherwise have done. But these papers will come into the hands of such. To them I particularly recommend and dedicate this relation. Oh, my dear young friends, had you seen with what dignity of spirit she filled up the last scene of her life, you must have been affected by it! Let not the liveliness of your spirits, and the gayety of the prospect around you, prevent you from considering, that to you likewise, days will certainly come, unless you are suddenly snatched out of life, when you will say and feel that the world, and all in it, can afford you no pleasure. But there is a Saviour, Jesus Christ, a Mighty One, always near, always gracious to those who seek him. May you, like her, be enabled to choose him as the Guide of your youth, and the Lord of your hearts. Then, like her, you will find support and comfort under affliction, wisdom to direct your conduct, a good hope in death, and by death a happy translation to everlasting life.

I have only to add my prayers that a blessing from on high may descend upon the persons and families of all my friends, and upon all into whose hands this paper may providentially come.

John Newton

Amazing Grace

by John Newton
Olney Hymns (London: W. Oliver, 1799)

Amazing grace! How sweet the sound
That saved a wretch like me!
I once was lost, but now am found;
Was blind, but now I see.

'Twas grace that taught my heart to fear,
And grace my fears relieved;
How precious did that grace appear
The hour I first believed.

Through many dangers, toils and snares,
I have already come;
'Tis grace hath brought me safe thus far,
And grace will lead me home.

The Lord has promised good to me,
His Word my hope secures;
He will my Shield and Portion be,
As long as life endures.

Yea, when this flesh and heart shall fail,
And mortal life shall cease,
I shall possess, within the veil,
A life of joy and peace.

The earth shall soon dissolve like snow,
The sun forbear to shine;
But God, Who called me here below,
Shall be forever mine.

When we've been there ten thousand years,
Bright shining as the sun,
We've no less days to sing God's praise
Than when we'd first begun.

To order additional copies of

Letters and Reflections
to My Adopted Daughters

Have your credit card ready and call:

1-877-421-READ (7323)

or please visit our web site at
www.pleasantword.com

Also available at:
www.amazon.com
and
www.barnesandnoble.com

Printed in the United States
25718LVS00001B/183

9 781414 102641